GULF OF MEXICO

TENNESSEE

ARKANSAS

Mississippi

• Memphis

MISSISSIPPI

LOUISIANA

• Vicksburg

Natchez
•

St. Francisville
•

Baton Rouge
★

New Orleans
•

N E S W

Mississippi

By Diane Siebert

ILLUSTRATED BY

Greg Harlin

HARPERCOLLINSPUBLISHERS

To the people of the river who shared with me their knowledge and

love of the Mississippi, and to my husband, Bob, who cheers me on

—D.S.

To the memory of my mother, Polly Harlin

—G.H.

Mississippi
Text copyright © 2001 by Diane Siebert
Illustrations copyright © 2001 by Greg Harlin
Printed in the United States of America.
All rights reserved.
www.harperchildrens.com

Library of Congress Cataloging-in-Publication Data
Siebert, Diane.
 Mississippi / Diane Siebert ; illustrated by
Greg Harlin.
  p.   cm.
 ISBN 0-688-16445-5
 ISBN 0-688-16446-3 (lib. bdg.)
 1. Mississippi River—Juvenile literature.
[1. Mississippi River.]   I. Harlin, Greg, ill.
II. Title.
F351.S45   2001   00-38902
976.2—dc21   CIP
                                                         AC

        1 2 3 4 5 6 7 8 9 10
                        ❖
                  First Edition

I am the river,

Deep and strong.

I sing an old, enduring song

With rhythms wild and rhythms tame,

And Mississippi is my name.

From ice and snow my life began
As melting glacial waters ran
In rising, frigid floods that found
A thousand paths to lower ground.

And where these many paths converged,
Their channeled waters rose and surged
Down through the land, creating me—
A river, young and wild and free.

Time rolled along, and so did I—
A part of untamed earth and sky—
At one with reptiles, fish, and birds;
With mammoths, sloths, and bison herds.

A thousand years. Then thousands more
Brought sounds I had not heard before.
The sounds were voices, strange and new,
Now moving ever closer to
These waters that would soon reflect
The shapes of those who walk erect.

For as the human family spread
It reached my banks to lightly tread
These hunting grounds, these fertile lands,
As primitive, nomadic bands.
They drank from me, used spears of stone,
And worked with tools of wood and bone.

Then came the dugout and canoe
Of Choctaw, Winnebago, Sioux;
Of Chicasaw and Illinois.
They honored me. I sang with joy.

And then from Spain and France they came—
Explorers who would stake their claim
And battle for this new frontier.
I felt their presence grow each year.

Time passed. The native tribes lost ground
To those whose flatboats, southward bound,
Gave way to keelboats poled upstream
And paddle wheelers run by steam.

I watched this European tide;
It pushed the native world aside
As settlers, towns, and roads appeared;
As farms sprang up; as land was cleared.

The quiet days had surely passed
With changes coming hard and fast.
I heard the mighty gunboats roar
Amid a bloody civil war,
Then watched the country, torn in two,
Be reunited, born anew.

What followed was a nation's quest
To grow, expand, and "tame" the West.
Then came the impact of the train—
I felt my river traffic wane
Till World War I brought increased trade;
Upon me, vessels now conveyed
A wealth of goods moved by the ton.
Another era had begun.

I watched a modern nation grow.
I listened and have come to know
Each boat and ship from stem to stern
Whose mechanized propellers turn
And whose soft sonar voices speak
Beneath my surface as they seek
The obstacles within myself—
The sandbar, snag, and rocky shelf.

I know the constant push and pull
Of towboats with their barges full;
The boats for fishing and for sport
That fill the slips in every port;
The Coast Guard tenders placing buoys;
The river towns, the lights, the noise.

And at each straightaway and curve
I see the people whom I serve,
Whose commerce and whose industry
Depend on what I've come to be:
A resource, now at their command;
A lifeline stretching through the land.

Yet growth and change exact a cost,
And nature's gifts are often lost
When humans, through their greed and haste,
Pollute and poison me with waste.
For now my muddy water hides
The garbage, sludge, and pesticides
That kill my fish and fowl to find
Their lethal way back to mankind.

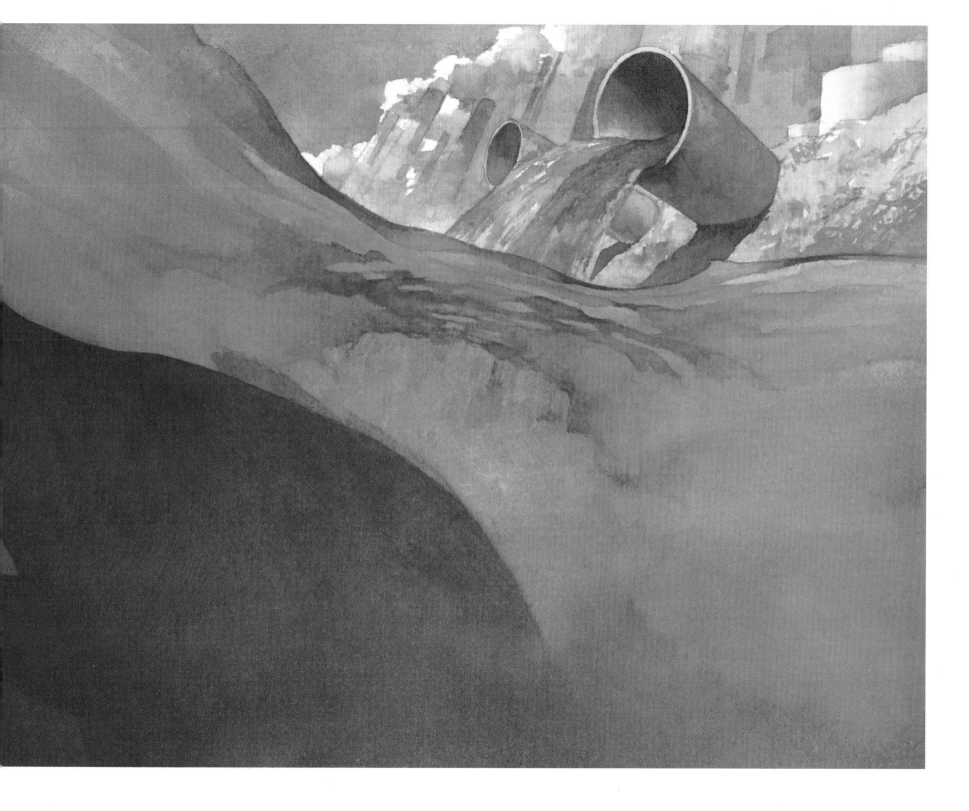

I am the river,

Touched by Man

Whose steel and concrete bridges span

These waters lined with ports and docks,

Restrained by levees, dams, and locks,

And shaped by dredges as they keep

My shifting channel wide and deep.

And yet, in spite of these controls,

My raging floods, my hidden shoals,

My course that changes day to day,

My theft of silt and sand and clay

Attest to forces, never curbed,

That leave the human world disturbed;

These forces sing an old refrain.

They tell of loss; they tell of gain.

They leave this message in their wake:

These waters give.

These waters take.

I am the river.
Come with me
And know my journey to the sea
As, cold and clear, I wander forth
From Lake Itasca in the north
Where water carves its bright designs
Upon the earth, amid the pines.

Here as a tiny creek I start
My journey through the nation's heart;
And fed by streams and lakes I grow
As north, then east, then south I flow
To Minneapolis and St. Paul
Where, strong and sure and swift, I fall
In currents harnessed for their might,
Creating power, heat, and light.

Then hugged by limestone bluffs that guide

My passage through the countryside,

My quiet currents move between

Rock Island, Davenport, Moline;

Past maples, oaks, and hickories—

The forests of the hardwood trees;

And past the farms and fields that lie

Beneath the broad midwestern sky.

Then dreaming dreams of long ago,

On down to Hannibal I flow,

Where happy memories remain

Of steamboats, and a man called Twain.

And I, the river, ever blessed
By waters from the east and west,
Now feel the great Missouri bring
Its music to the song I sing.
This river, Rocky Mountain–born,
Flows down past farms and fields of corn,
And near St. Louis, where we meet,
Its muddy rhythms, swift and sweet,
Unite with mine, and on we run—
Two mighty rivers, joined as one.

While from the east, from high plateaus,

The beautiful Ohio flows

To meet me, as do countless more;

And as these tributaries pour

Into me, all along my length,

They give to me their gathered strength

And tell me tales of history

While whispering their names to me:

    The Wyaconda and the Crow.

    The Wolf, the Bear, the Buffalo.

    The Illinois, the Arkansas.

    The Rock, the Red, the Chippewa.

I know them all and where they've been,

And faithfully I take them in,

Becoming deep, a mile-wide force

In conflict with a twisted course.

And touching Memphis, Tennessee,

I wind toward Vicksburg restlessly.

Down through the deep green South I spill—

Past Natchez …

          Past St. Francisville …

And fighting every loop and bend,

I cut new channels that extend

Into a watery terrain—

The ever-changing coastal plain,

Where, just as they once joined with me,

Rebellious currents now break free;

Where bayous draped in Spanish moss

Are formed and nourished by my loss.

This is a place of swamps and lakes;

Of alligators, birds, and snakes;

Of misty light on grays and greens;

Of Baton Rouge and New Orleans.

Then through diverging paths I flow

Into the Gulf of Mexico,

Now laden with the soil and sand

That I have stolen from the land.

And slowed by waves that clash with me,

I leave my burden to the sea,

While endless currents, cool and brown,

Keep rolling on …

　　　　　Keep rolling down.…

I am the river,

Wide and deep,

Whose restless waters never sleep;

And as I move with currents strong,

I sing an old, enduring song

With rhythms wild and rhythms tame.

And Mississippi is my name.

About the River

It is powerful and majestic, a river of creation and destruction. Native American tribes that once lived and hunted along this great ribbon of water called it *Messipi*, which means "big water" or "father of waters." It was a good name.

Beginning in Minnesota's Lake Itasca as a stream only a few inches deep and a few feet across, it rolls down through the heart of America for 2,350 miles, collecting water from its hundreds of tributaries and growing in width to a mile and a half at its widest point. With its tributaries it forms a drainage system of approximately 1,250,000 square miles, draining all or part of thirty-one U.S. states and two Canadian provinces. Each day it discharges about 400 billion gallons of water into the Gulf of Mexico. Each year it carries off 495 million tons of soil and sand, which it deposits into the sea. It is used by thousands of vessels to ship millions of tons of freight annually.

It is the Mississippi.

River Words

buoy: an anchored floating device, sometimes carrying a light, whistle, or bell, marking a channel or obstruction lying beneath the water

channel: the bed of a waterway, usually the deepest part

coastal plain: the flat, often swampy margin of land at the southeastern edge of the United States

dam: a barrier that obstructs and controls the flow of water

dredge: to scoop mud from the bottom of a river

levee: an embankment for preventing a river from overflowing its banks

lock: an enclosed portion of a river, with a gate at each end, for controlling the water level and for raising and lowering vessels from one level to another

rocky shelf: an outcropping of rock

sandbar: a ridge of sand formed in a river by the action of water currents

shoal: a shallow place in a body of water

silt: fine particles of rock and soil suspended in and carried by water

slip: a space between two wharves or in a dock, for boats to lie in

sludge: a deposit of ooze at the bottom of a body of water, produced by sewage

snag: an obstacle, such as the trunk of a tree, fixed in the bottom of a river and presenting a danger to navigation

tributary: a stream or river flowing into a larger stream or river